Soul Process

Paul E. McAtarsney

ISBN:1494201232
ISBN-13:9781494201234

DEDICATI★N

This book is dedicated to my Soul Mate, Margorie. Who daily encouraged me in the writing of this book and completion of other projects. Without your help and loving support, this may never have come to pass. Grateful for you in my life.

~ Paul E.

C✪NTENTS

ACKNOWLEDGMENTS

A Big thank you to all my friends who, through their love and support, help me see the light at the end of the tunnel.

T o all the people who, on a daily and even moment to moment basis, choose love.

T o the people whose daily experience is mainly darkness. Know that darkness cannot be where love abides.

> *"For eons our society has been suppressed and controlled. Now is the time for all that is true to come to light, all that is hidden to be revealed. This book is about being that light, being that truth. As each one of us embraces our truth and becomes it, lives it, we all rise together and take the next step in humanity's evolution."*

> *~ Paul E. McAtarsney*

INTRODUCTION

"The unforgiving mind is full of fear, and offers love no room to be itself; no place where it can spread its wings in peace and soar above the turmoil of the world. The unforgiving mind is sad, without the hope of respite and release from pain. It suffers and abides in misery, peering about in darkness, seeing not, yet certain of the danger lurking there.

The unforgiving mind is torn with doubt, confused about itself and all it sees; afraid and angry, weak and blustering, afraid to go ahead, afraid to stay, afraid to waken or to go to sleep, afraid of every sound, yet more afraid of stillness; terrified of darkness, yet more terrified at the approach of light. What can the unforgiving mind perceive but its damnation? What can it behold except the proof that all its sins are real?

The unforgiving mind sees no mistakes, but only sins. It looks upon the world with sightless eyes, and shrieks as it beholds its own projections rising to attack its miserable parody of life. It wants to live, yet wishes it were dead. It wants forgiveness, yet it sees no hope. It wants escape, yet can conceive of none because it sees the sinful everywhere.

The unforgiving mind is in despair, without the prospect of a future which can offer anything but more despair. Yet it regards its judgement of the world as irreversible, and does not see it has condemned itself to this despair. It thinks it cannot change, for what it sees bears witness that its judgement is correct. It does not ask, because it thinks it knows. It does not question, certain it is right..."

The unforgiving mind... Lesson 121

~ A Course In Miracles ~

7

Some thirty years ago when I first started on this journey I'd have given anything for a central point of reference that would point me to easily accessible tools of enlightenment. The Author does not claim that this book includes every single tool available; simply that when the reader has finished he/she will be in a much more empowered position from where to begin the journey.

This book is about providing the reader with a collection of powerful tools that are easy to use and highly practical. There are lots of people selling these tools as either collections or as standalone products. Refer to your powerful intuition in such matters, but there is a plethora of information to be found via the internet and other sources on all forms of healing.

After using the tools in this book, maybe investigate some more; the techniques, the common threads that connect them all. Take it a step deeper and feel what to do next. We are always given just what we require, so if you are reading this book, you are ready to take the next step.

Remember: lessons cannot be taught. they have to be experienced. Information and knowledge have no power unless they are put into action and it is in the doing that we push our boundaries. It is in the acts of love that we expand and become more. How can I serve others? How can I be more love? These are the ways to grow, to become more. There is a phase for knowing all I can about love and then there is a blossoming into being love. Being love in every moment, feeling, thought, word and deed.

While the search I embarked on proved invaluable to me

for many reasons; the time has now come for Man to take a quantum step forward in development. Not one or two but all of us awaking from slumber and seeing the truth of all that is. Embracing that truth and all that it means. Taking responsibility for the changes that must be made and choosing all of these steps together as a race.

Look around at what we are doing to the very environment that sustains us. We poison the earth we stand on. We pollute the oceans. Destroy life giving forests. Treat beautiful animals, birds, and insects and fish as if they have no worth.

We allow seventeen thousand children a day to starve and then shrug it off because no one else seems to care. As a society we ignore daily atrocities and speak unkindly in defence of self when challenged. This sense of disconnect from each other and all that is, this separateness, is at the core of the illusion, the vast majority of people share on a daily basis.

Very few people's actions live up to their belief system. People may profess many loving things, enthuse about their divine assignment on earth, and yet, their daily behaviour is far from loving.

Day to day, the civilised world sits around boxes and watches flashing images of falsehood and illusion, which aid in the deception that everything is wonderful, when in reality our society is clearly far from healthy.
Would be masters pull the strings of deception in the background. All they do are designed to assure the masses don't awake. They fear that day because when it happens and it is surely happening, their days of power are at an end.

One way or another, those days are gone. Humanity is changing.

Within the next ten years, we as a race, will implode and infamously and silently recede into history or we explode higher in consciousness, embracing all in love. I favour the latter option.

As you read, understand and try the tools listed in this book, you may find that you prefer one tool over the others. This is normal and at times you will find that you naturally feel drawn towards one tool or for a period of time only utilise a certain set of processing tools.

You will also see in certain circumstances that certain tools are more appropriate than others in that moment or during that period of your life. Follow your intuition and your inner guidance as to which tools to use.

Keep processing. Keep transmuting dark to light, fear to love. Keep moving forward and building up the momentum, until the day comes when you tip the scales in favour of love.

At that point your reality, your energy will be more about light than dark and that's where you will experience significant change.

That's not to say that you wait for positive change to come and only expect to get it at that point. If you do that, you will always be waiting for "that point" and then the next "that point" and your reality will always be about waiting before things improve. So, it's important to expect good things now.

The truth is this: your reality is abundant in all things.

Abundant in love, money, health. Abundant in so many ways. Keep the faith and keep putting one step in front of the next. Pick a tool, and process at least once a day. Meditate every morning and afternoon, or at least once a day.

If you connect in the morning, God will guide you the rest of the day and all you have to do is listen.

Praying is so very powerful; bless everything you can, bless every one you can, every circumstance and have faith that you are in God's hands and how can anything that you experience not be perfect?

God is here to support and protect you every step of the way. If you do have any fear regarding this or anything, simply process and release it. Transmute it to love.

This is an abundant, loving, sharing, giving universe that wants to help you and everyone else. Trust that's the case, trust that everything is working with you and that God is fully supporting you. All you have to do is believe and choose him. Stand in your power by being someone of integrity, by being who you are meant to be, who you really are. Speak your truth. If something is wrong, say it's wrong, but do it with love or say nothing at all. Do nothing at all if not with love.

You can have an opinion but never force your views on someone else. Allow things to be as they are and ultimately you may choose to do nothing in a circumstance or you may choose to act, but either way always coming from a place of love, the way is always love.

If you are ever fearful, process it, transmute it to love and re-evaluate. Speak your truth. It's not about being mean when you speak but like all true things, speaking your truth always comes from a place of love. When speaking your truth, you are never out to hurt or harm anyone. If you find yourself in a negative circumstance you may choose to say something or you may choose not to, depending on how your intuition guides you in that moment; trust that guidance. Intuition always comes from love.

You have a life compass that guides, directs and tells you what's fearful and what's loving. Anything fearful is coming from your ego and in that simple recognition is transmuted and anything loving that feels good should be grabbed, and you should go with that, because that's your intuition that's always pointing in the direction of love, always love.

A situation may add up on paper but your gut feeling, your intuition may be saying no. Always follow your life compass. No matter what your mind may advise, love is always the right choice.

For your life path, your journey, always choose truth, always peace, always joy and Love. There's never a need to do anything at the expense of another. Even if sometimes it means walking away, there is always a loving solution.

Above all else be true, be yourself. Learn the tools in this book. Study them through other sources, ignore some, find others. Embrace change. You have a simple moment to moment choice, Fear or Love.

Making any choice is better than no choice and whatever choice you make is the right choice because you made it. You intuitively know what the right choice is. Make one and it's guaranteed to be the right one but you have to make a choice.
When you've chosen, follow it through. Put aside any doubts you may have and Go for it! You always have the option of choosing again at a later stage. Choose love and simply allow this year to be everything you've ever dreamed of.

SUBCONSCIOUS

"The function of the mind is to create coherence between our beliefs and the reality we experience," Dr. Lipton said. "What that means is that your mind will adjust the body's biology and behavior to fit with your beliefs. If you've been told you'll die in six months and your mind believes it, you most likely will die in six months. That's called the nocebo effect, the result of a negative thought, which is the opposite of the placebo effect, where healing is mediated by a positive thought.

That dynamic points to a three-party system: there's the part of you that swears it doesn't want to die (the conscious mind), trumped by the part that believes you will (the doctor's prognosis mediated by the subconscious mind), which then throws into gear the chemical reaction (mediated by the brain's chemistry) to make sure the body conforms to the dominant belief.

Neuroscience has recognized that the subconscious controls 95 percent of our lives."

~ Dr Bruce Lipton

The part of our psyche that most people ignore on a day to day basis, the subconscious never stops, is always active. Even when we are asleep it is processing, being and creating our reality. It is of paramount importance to work with and clear any blockages that may be there.

For me removing energy blocks, resistance and negative patterns is the most powerful use of processing. These blocks prevent us from having all the good that should be in our lives. We "live in a "*hurricane of grace....*" as *Abraham Hicks* states.
The Universe wants us to have and do and be everything we desire! We are the ones who stop it coming to us.

Okay, I hear you thinking. I would never do that! Why would I stop the good in my life coming to me? Short answer is, most folk are not aware that they are blocking or resisting good coming into their lives.

Maybe as a child you continually heard "we can't afford that" or "do you think I'm a Millionaire!?" or something similar from your parents. They always turned off the lights and turned down the heating to save money.

Over time and through the natural law of Entrainment, these and other negative patterns and actions caused the formation of these energy blockages in you, the one above being a block to abundance. These blocks keep you from having the things you want in life.

Including: Health, Money, Abundance and Love.

ENTRAINMENT

"In physics, entrainment has been used to refer to the process of mode locking of coupled driven oscillators, which is the process whereby two interacting oscillating systems, which have different periods when they function independently, assume a common period. The two oscillators may fall into synchrony, but other phase relationships are also possible. The system with the greater frequency slows down, and the other speeds up. Dutch physicist Christian Huygens, the inventor of the pendulum clock, introduced the concept after he noticed, in 1666, that the pendulums of two clocks mounted on a common board had synchronized, and subsequent experiments duplicated this phenomenon..."

Source
http://en.wikipedia.org/wiki/Entrainment_(phys ics)

We are all 100% energy as is everything in the universe. Everything we perceive as solid is energy and can be seen as such if you delve deep enough.

Because of this well-known scientific fact, other energies can have an effect on us and this truth can also be explained by science as the law of Entrainment.

Some examples of entrainment:

- ∞ women who live together often get their periods at the same time
- ∞ while meditating you feel a more profound deeper experience
- ∞ while at a concert you feel "caught up" in the music
- ∞ in the company of a negative person you feel drained

Question: When you are surrounded by negativity and folk are saying energetically, be like us or we don't like you! What do you do?

Answer: At that point you have a choice to make and life is all about choices. This one entails you deciding whether allowing yourself to be bullied into being negative and buying into the drama of your associates is the right thing or sticking to what you know is truth and assisting yourself and your friends.

For me there's no choice here. By reaching for the best in everything, every time, you not only help yourself by keeping your vibration high but you also help your friends whether they recognize it or not by pulling their vibration up. This is the law of entrainment at work.

If your friend is someone who continually brings you down I suggest you have some alone time, often!

"Unexpressed emotions will never die. They are buried alive and will come forth later in uglier ways." ~ Sigmund Freud

Stay in "Presence" when around your friend. When you are the observer of your thoughts, you cannot be pulled into drama or triggered to react. When you react, you add your negative energy to theirs.

What's happening is that when a person strikes out at us because of their pain, they sub consciously know just where to direct their energy to get the best reaction. It's part of what we are here for, to help each other in that way, by pointing out where we require work on ourselves to happen.

I've discussed the dynamics of how we learn from these and other interactions in my section on Lessons and Mirrors later in this book.

Learning to practice mindfulness during all of your day is also a wonderful way of slowing down. Maybe there's a park close to your work place?
How about lunch in the Sun, Entraining to the nurturing rhythm of Nature?

Working in today's hectic society has most people's internal clocks running at too high a pace. We are not designed to run at one hundred per cent twenty four seven and sadly that what happens to most of us on a day to day basis.

Basically, we use more energy when we are not in sync with the surrounding energy and less when we are.
If you need to speed up to the pace of your work, that's okay, as long as you slow down when it's completed. That's also about grabbing slices of time during your work day to slow down, a quick meditation or "power nap" when appropriate. I know from my own experience in a fast paced job, that breaking it up with down time put me in a more productive mode after.

Society has a way of pulling us into a faster pace, but remember, you always have a choice.
And while you do have the ability to choose, choice is something you can't properly make until you awake.

Until then everything you do, every action and seemingly free choice you make is simply a reaction to stimuli and as a consequence of programming.
Choose to be aware, firstly of your own energy and slow down. To entrain to nature and to your natural pace. Protect your energy when necessary but always come from a place of love, when you do.

PROGRAMMING BY SOCIETY

The people who are in control of society know that you are a powerful creator. So they program you through, the media, TV, radio, papers, books, movies, schools, health, and work. Every facet of society is setup to control what you create. I mention this because it's good to be aware of how you are being controlled so you can step into your birth right and your power. This awareness also allows you to see what you don't want in your life. When you know what you don't want that shows you what you do want and you can start focusing on and creating the stuff you prefer to see more of in your reality.

Ever notice when you start the day in a negative way it seems to get worse as the day proceeds? Well that works the same with beginning your day in a positive way too. Begin the day with a smile on your face. Be grateful for what you already have and expect good things to come to you. They will!

When you process one of the changes is your perception of reality. Think of it like polishing your reading glasses. Processing allows you to see things as they really are. The more you process, the more you spiritually become aware of. You gain easier access to your guidance for a start. Inner wisdom, awareness, joy and deep love are your birth right and with processing they are permanently with you.

Some people have said to me that they need anger to

achieve anything in their life. It's the anger that gives them that extra push to get over the hill and to reach their goals.

My truth is that all negativity is illusion. All illusion is lies. Your ego, as the father of lies, wants you to believe anger is useful. But in truth, it is not. All things come and go, are born and die. Only you are eternal.

You are not separate from anything. "We are all One" is more than a beautiful catchphrase; it's an accurate description of the nature of Ultimate Reality.

Motivation fueled from anger will fade as all things pass but motivation coming from love is eternal and without end. Anything negative and from illusion will exist and then disappear. Only Peace, joy and love are eternal. These are eternal because they spring from deep inside. These states of being cannot be found in outside things. Only in looking deep inside will you find eternal Peace, Joy and Love of God. Why will you find them deep inside you, simply because you are God?

When you process, leave all your expectations behind. You will be surprised about what will appear for it to be released. I've seen energies of an old man, numerous Dragons of various sizes and colors; A dog, horses, cats and rabbits. Have seen numerous past life experiences, especially how they ended. Endings for me were always traumatic and bloody; Swords, Hatchets, Spears, Maces, Hooves, Lions, Sharks, Tigers. All these things have been in my energy. They were energetic memories still affecting my energy and thus the way I interacted with my reality, in this life time.

Remember, you are always supported by the angels when you call them in. Angels are the messengers of God.

If you don't remember to call them, it's okay as well. If you do, it's okay and if you don't, it's okay.

Thing is, most people can't see the bigger picture. That's true with anything they do or don't do in life. If you take action, it's okay and if you don't take action, it's still okay because that's the action you took at the time. Whatever you choose IS the right action; for you. You can only be concerned with action that concerns you. What others do or don't do is their choice, their path.

Example: You see an empty can lying on the ground. Should you pick it up or should you walk past? The same applies. It's okay either way. You don't see the bigger picture and have no way of knowing what will happen if you pick up the can or leave it there.

Is it your responsibility to pick the can up? It is if you believe it is. Are you picking it up because you are making that decision based on love or are you picking it up because of fear? That can be your only guide. If it's fear, then it's your ego and you should leave it there. If its love and your intuition, pick it up because that should always be your guidance. Always come from a place of love.

Maybe that Can is a sermon to someone else? Maybe it lying on the ground is a catalyst for change to someone else who sees it laying there? We don't walk someone else's path and are only responsible for our own. Remember that whether you do or don't, it's always the right thing. It's always the right thing because we live in a reality of perfection, so how could it be otherwise?

When you first try anything new it can seem difficult and maybe even impossible but keep going and the way will become clear to you. Keep processing and coming from love in all things.

Society will do its best to convince you that all is negative and life is without hope or respite. Everything is setup to help you come to that conclusion but the truth is that the opposite of that state is true.

Life is about cooperation, joy, peace, abundance and love. When you start to put the tools in this book into practice, you will see the truth in that statement. When you come to a place of enough awareness and start manifesting from a place of stillness, joy and love; never mind what society states; you WILL create Heaven on Earth for you.

It's never been about anyone else. It's always about you. No matter what "the facts" say, you create everything in your reality. Everything! That's why the "powers that be" want you in a place of perpetual fear. You are so much more controllable there as opposed to standing in your power and creating an abundant loving reality.

SPEAK YOUR TRUTH

'The word "integrity" stems from the Latin adjective integer, (whole, complete).In this context, integrity is the inner sense of "wholeness" deriving from qualities such as honesty and consistency of character. As such, one may judge that others "have integrity" to the extent that they act according to the values, beliefs and principles they claim to hold.' ~ Wikipedia

Now is the time for radical truth. Truth with yourself, truth about your life, your path, your health, truth about who you are, truth about every facet of your reality. Why is it so difficult and radical to be 100% honest? When you are honest and truthful about anything you are shining a powerful light upon the darkness of lies and deception. Yes, deceiving, lying and believing lies to feel better, will not serve anyone, especially you.

Why are so many concerned with what friends or society thinks? Your critics will play that role and your allies will always be what they are. What does it matter? Nothing anyone says or does is important. It's your feelings, words and actions that are. It's your thoughts and emotions that create everything in your reality. Take responsibility as you are the creator of everything you consider bad or good in your life.

Speaking your truth is not about being hurtful or

judgmental it's about saying what is true for you and allowing others to do what is right for them.

Want your life to change then look at yourself, every facet of your life with the clear eyes of love.
What is it that doesn't feel good? Change it! What is it that does feel good? Do more of it! Change cannot start until the deception ends. Be kind, be truthful be the real you, be love.

Something in society bothering you? Don't like some thing in politics? Don't ignore it, change it. Why vote for a party because it's who your father voted for or your friends vote for? Exercise your power and vote for what feels right.

Some have asked, what's the difference between a mask and a persona? A mask is something that people put in front of them because they are in a place of fear. Fear maybe of simply being judged. Judging always says more about the person judging and is never about the judged.

A persona is the opposite polarity of a mask and is when someone stands in their power, maybe for example speaking their truth as a spiritual teacher or teacher in general and are tapping into their main strength depending on the circumstance.

You have all the power. All it takes is enough of us deciding to be truthful about who and what we are. Start with speaking the truth about what, from a loving perspective matters to you. Then choose to stand in your power. Watch the facade of lies come tumbling down. Washed away by the clear, honest, shining light of truth.

Our society is changing for the better. Every day we see examples of this enlightening change. More information being released; full disclosure of the U.F.O phenomena, cures for diseases discussed in main stream media.

Monumental change is upon us. No need to be afraid. All change is good. When something in your life is taken away from you, is it really about loss? Maybe what's happening is space being created for better things to come into your reality.

Like all things you have a choice. You have the power over how you perceive and that choose is always negative or positive.

Speak your truth, first to yourself, then to all you encounter. Always from a place of love.

You are standing in your power when you speak your truth, come from a place of love and integrity in all things, follow your intuition and live the life of your dreams.

Trust that you are divinely guided and protected in all ways; you are. There is great power in simply reaching for the good of all things whether it's a feeling, thought, action or situation. When you are in this way, authentic, you tap into the power of the Universe. The power that you are, is the same power that creates and manages the planets and all life in the most perfect way.

Want things in your life to change for the better? Be authentic; choose to harness the power of the Universe. Choose to be the real you and coming from a place of love, speak your truth.

WHAT YOU BELIEVE IS TRUE

Was chatting with a friend of mine the other day, who was saying that she has quit coffee, sugar and smoking all in the same time. She had a headache and was obviously detoxing. Natural enough! I totally agree that removing toxins from her energy is definitely a wonderful loving thing to do.

Part way through the discussion I mentioned that, as she controls everything in her reality, she didn't have to quit any of these if she could believe that they weren't bad for her. Irritated by this remark she promptly informed me that she was going and did so.

My truth is this. We indeed create our own reality. We co-create joint realities with others. What we "Believe" IS true!

We live in a society where we've been taught how to act, think and behave. An Original thought is frowned upon and every part of our society is designed to control and manipulate us. Once you start to awake and look around you start to see the truth.

Part of that truth is that you control your reality. You can have and do and be ... anything you wish. That is your true Power. That is your ultimate truth!
But wait, I could, for example state, "I'm now a millionaire!" Poof, My room is chockablock full of money! Hmm well no, that won't work! I say the words but

there's resistance or negativity to that statement and that's all it is a statement. Resistance in what way you may ask?

When you were a child, your parents were always fighting over money. Or there never was enough for them. They were just not content or grateful for what they had and always were in a lack way of thinking and being. This energy was transferred to you in the form of a pattern and now you have a block to money and abundance flowing into your life. So no matter how much you say "I'm now a millionaire!" You will never be, because at an energetic level you don't believe it's possible!

That's just one scenario of countless possibilities where you could have accumulated resistance. This resistance leaves you energetically, standing in a hurricane of Bliss and abundance with your hands up shouting NO! No to abundance, no to happiness, no to love and no to all the "good" stuff that you want in your life.

What to do? Firstly, recognize that there is a blockage and then create your own tool belt full of processing tools you can use whenever there is a need. Just select the appropriate tool, whether it's E.F.T, Meditation, Mindfulness or any other form of processing. Removing resistance to what you want and then becoming the energy of what you want is a sure fire way to get what it is you desire.

LIFE'S A BOWL OF FRUIT

Do you ever notice when you are eating? Let's say a bowl of fruit. You put your fork into a slice of pineapple and go to pick it up; it slips off! This happens a few times before you finally get it to stay on the fork. Then you have the enjoyment of putting it into your mouth. All the yummy tastes, sensations and general good feel associated with something you love to eat.

Well, maybe navigating through life is just like that and there's a couple of ways to look at this.
We could keep trying to pick up a slice of fruit over and over until we finally get it in our mouths or we could refine our technique so we pick up the fruit every time.

What about maybe going with the flow of eating?
When we first try to pick up a slice of apple; it falls off our fork. We try a slice of pear; that falls off. A piece of pineapple stays on and we gratefully munch it! Yum.

Isn't it possible that pineapple is the fruit we were meant to eat in the first place? Not the Apple at all!

What happens in life happened and couldn't have happened any other way, because it happened.
We can't see the bigger picture of our lives but God does. He sees all and knows all and from his perspective that piece of Apple just wasn't going to work for you, so he guided you to a piece of Pineapple!

Now the cool thing is that God made you in his image. You are God and God is you! It's God guiding you to the pineapple but it's also you guiding you to what's in your highest good.

See; you have all the answers. All the knowledge all the power, all the love, all the peace and all the joy you can ever wish for. Thing is, you can't see it from where you are. From your perspective and this is the case for most people. From your perspective it's all dark out there. That's because most people choose to look at life from the perspective of fear. They make this sub conscious choice because they've been programmed by society as a method of control.

For those who choose to see life from the perspective of Love and reach for the good in all things, know that Love transforms if you choose to allow it.

Love within transforms the world around us.   As we observe all around us with the eyes of love, all we are aware of is transformed to the best it can be in that moment. Choose to give love and to see all around from a perspective of love. When you give love you receive love. It's the Law of attraction at work.

Choose to love yourself; it's not selfish to do so. In fact by doing so you put yourself in a better place to give and receive love. What you give out to the Universe is what you receive. The Law of Attraction never stops working. This law works for everyone, all the time, everywhere, without fail! Love everyone you can. Love everything you can. Love with all that you are! Choose LOVE!

In a universe of duality, black/white, Ying/Yang, negative/positive, birth/death; all of these polarities serve in providing us with Choice. Where what we think and feel creates our reality. In this universe when you think negative thoughts you create a negative reality and positivity creates a positive reality. I have to ask you; is there really a choice?
We are all choosing moment to moment and fear will always bring negativity while love will bring more things to love.

We live in a universe of unending love and abundance. Choose to allow love into your energy. Decide that this is the year for love in your life. From now on beginning this moment your life is about love and how to transpose what you feel into actions. Actions that show others by your example and by your energy, what the true meaning of life is about!
Being happy now, being joy now! Life is for living and living is expanding. Expanding via our experiences.

All things have a beginning and an end. Are born and will die. There are large cycles like the cycles of the universe which measured by the Myan's stretched to 25,000 years to the life of a mayfly, which can be a day. Everywhere we look there are wheels within wheels, beginnings and endings. It's the natural order of things.
    Remember the things that come into your life that you don't want show you clearly what you do want! Everything serves a purpose! You teach or learn every moment in your life. Enjoy, love and allow the universe to fully support you in every way. Life is meant to be abundant in every way! Choose to Allow, Choose love!

Life is full of lessons. Even in a bowl of fruit there's a lesson and possibly many more for those with eyes to see. That simply means; those who ask to see.

In any case, enjoy eating your bowl of fruit. It's a moment to moment choice to enjoy bite after tasty bite. Are there limits to how many bowls you can have? The only limits are the ones you create. This particular meal is limitless, boundless and endless.
As you are!

BOUNDARIES

For me a spiritual boundary may be thought of as a limit to what is considered allowable in your reality. Some examples might be, saying No to behavior, circumstances or situations. The action of saying no would involve a judgment for the ego or a discernment of the soul.

A boundary can be a useful tool to be used when deemed necessary. Maybe along your evolution you may discern that a boundary is important to institute until you've grown enough not to require one in a given situation, for example.

Let's say there's a person who simply triggers patterns of behavior in you that are not acceptable. A boundary is a wonderful method of controlling when and where you retrain and process your reaction to such an extent where a boundary is no longer required. The more you process a reaction in your energy to any negativity or situation, the less you will react to it and in time you won't react at all. When you are in that place nothing including that person will be able to affect you and eventually they will simply not be in your reality.

For someone not aware of their path or spiritual journey, if asked the question, "what do you think of boundaries" , might choose to answer, "Why do I need boundaries?" They may never have heard of boundaries or their programmed boundaries and limits may prevent them via fear to consider any possibilities of more,
especially more love in their lives.
At the other end of the scale, a fully realized individual

might also answer the question of "what do you think of boundaries", if they answered at all, with, "why would I need boundaries?"

And indeed, why would they require boundaries if they are coming from a place of total peace, joy and unconditional love. Why would anyone require boundaries when fear is absent and they only know love.

GIVING

Over the years I have shared accommodation and or had a room in a house with shared utilities. Kitchen, bathroom, laundry services for example. I've found myself in a position where someone was using my shampoo and eating the food from a cupboard I used.

Initially this irked me a little bit, but because of the tools and the teaching I follow I was aware that this was a powerful lesson and a lesson in unconditional giving and ultimately in love.

This also raised questions about boundaries. Should I have boundaries at all, is there a need for a line and more separateness or should I simply give freely? What I decided after processing and feeling into this particular situation was to allow this individual to continue and to process any lack thinking on my part.

I came to this conclusion because, if I was to share and give, it should always be unconditional, as there are no limits or boundaries in unconditional love. God never gives us circumstances that we are not capable of coping with. We have all the answers, all the time, for every situation.

If there are any lack circumstances, and if I found myself in a place where I was without whatever it is I give, then it simply means that I am giving my powerful attention to lack instead of abundance and or I just don't require whatever it is I've given away and so should readjust my perspective. I'm eternally grateful for the powerful lesson and the opportunity to grow and be more love.

This is not to say, I will never find myself in a situation where I require boundaries. Discern what the right course of action is for you in each situation, until you reside in an energetic place of unconditional Love.

BE AWARE

It occurred to me while repairing my computer system one day, that unless I know what the issue is there is no way I will be able to rectify the situation.

In the same way, I have to know spiritually what needs correcting, whether it's an ingrained negative pattern in my life or in my thought processes.

Most people don't know there's a problem in their reality because of perspective, much in the same way as a fish in a bowl isn't aware of anything outside of the bowl. Having never experienced anything different, has nothing to compare what it has and so accepts what it has as the best it can ever have.

The same with most people, they may not be content with what they have in their reality but they have nothing to compare it with so they accept it. Meditation allows us to connect to our inner self. Being aware is simply about opening up to the idea of other possibilities. When you allow yourself to be open in this way, you allow change into your life. All change is good, as without change your energy and life becomes stagnant and without growth.

Embrace change when it arrives, in whatever form. With a simple change of perspective, everything that comes to you can be seen as good.

You can always find the good in every situation, circumstance and thing.

Let's say you have an argument with your boyfriend and he decides to leave. Or circumstances dictate that you leave. You set a boundary and while you don't feel so good about it, you know it's the right choice because you've followed your inner guidance and come to the decision from a place of love.

At this point, because you are aware, you know that all change is good. So instead of feeling remorseful and guilty, you are know that now having learned the lessons of the past relationship an even better one is coming to you.

Yes, it's possible, to find the good in every situation, with a simple change of heart.   From fear to Love.

INTUITION

What I call 'life compass', others may call 'Gut feeling' or 'Intuition'. This guidance is always divine and always comes from source. It is based on and comes only from love. Intuition flows from your "Higher Self", the part of you that sees and knows all. The you at a higher dimensional level, creating your reality and pointing you to circumstances of learning and spiritual growth.

I understand that life is intricate and often we are called on to make decisions and discernments'. Always follow your intuition. The trick here is being able to tell the difference between inner guidance and ego. Simply; if its love based its inner guidance and if it's not then it should be recognized, acknowledged and the only action should be to process any negativity associated with it.

There is a difference between discerning on a personal level, which is heartfelt and judging others. One you can and must do. One you should never do.

You discern all the time. When to rise in the morning, to sleep, what to eat, what to wear etc ... You have an inner knowing when something is right for you. This is your life compass pointing the way. Always follow it. It may not make sense in 3D world, but if your intuition is pointing that way, always go with it!

The law of attraction states that what we are is what we get more of in life. So, when you judge someone, you get judged. I personally only encourage and create loving energy in life.

One of the beautiful things about this reality is that we

always have a moment to moment choice. You get to judge or discern. You choose. No one else can choose for you.

Trust that when you've tuned your inner guidance and knowing; you'll always have a powerful tool for discerning the right path and making the right choice for you.

When you come to a fork in the road on your personal journey, you are always totally supported and guided when you listen by way of feeling to your Intuition.

AURA AND CHAKRAS

I will go into some detail about the aura and chakras which are part of your energy field. Your actual physical body is only a small part of your true self. What you see is not all there is. The human body is not just the blood and bones we perceive on the physical plane but is so much more. Stay open to possibilities.

We are made of 100% energy and this is what our beings consist of. What we know as the physical body is just slower vibrating energy that is connected to all that is. The aura or energy field is perceived by most people as invisible but nearly everyone can learn to recognize it in one way or another with practice. Further investigation of the aura and chakras is recommended and will be highly beneficial, especially when scanning your energy as you develop.

The aura is densest close to the body and becomes finer as we move away from it. Most Auras extend from One to Six feet out around the body, though in the more spiritually developed it can extend outward up to 40 feet from the body.

Disturbance and emotional trauma can create blocks and other damage in the energy body. If this damage is not repaired and continues to occur then over time the outward manifestation is disease and other forms of perceived resistance in your reality.

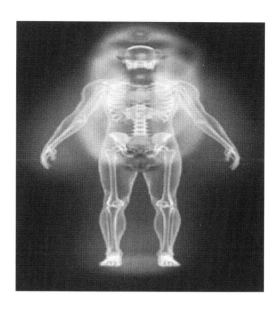

Each layer of the aura permeates the others and begins at the Chakra Centre.

The vibration of each level becomes finer and higher as we go from the inside out.

I'm one of the group of people who feel aura layers easier than seeing them, although I do see some colors. The aura color changes constantly depending on mood or how someone consistently thinks or believes and it may also have a principal color.

Size also varies, largely depending on the energy level of the person and the way they use that particular part of themselves. Stress, trauma and emotional pain can show as distortions and blocks in the aura, long before they manifest as illness. Each layer is classically related to one of seven chakras. Starting from the bottom up.

Root chakra; whose color is Red has a grayish layer that extends an inch or two out from the body most associated with the physical body is the easiest to see.

Sacral Chakra; whose color is orange, has a soft multi colored clouds of light visible from one to six inches out.

Solar Plexus; which is Yellow in color, is the mental body and reflects the thought processes, and personal power. Extends up to 12 inches from body.

These three bodies are the lower astral and together are said to make up the personality and to be created at conception and dissolve at death.

Heart chakra; Green color. This color may change to white. First of the spiritual layers, associated with the heart and love. This connects the lower three levels with the higher three. All healing energy comes through this layer. It is the layer of love.

Throat chakra; Blue in color. The higher aspects of the will as in connection with divine will, speech and communication, listening, taking responsibility for ones own actions. Extending about two and a half feet out from the body.

Third eye chakra; Purple color. Spiritual communication, divine Love fostering awareness of oneself as an aspect of what some call God, Love of all life and joining together. Becoming one.

Crown chakra; White color. Higher mind, connection with higher self and spiritual information and the integration of the spiritual and energetic aspects of being.

PROCESSING

"Energy cannot be created or destroyed, it can only be changed from one form to another"
~ Albert Einstein

Y ou are 100% energy.

Processing could be thought of as healing. Healing after all is a shift from fear to love. Processing using any of the tools described in this book does just that, transmutes negative energy to positive, fear to love.

It follows that harming, weakening, breaking is a move from love to fear. This sobering thought explains a lot of what we see happening in our society today. Our society after all is designed to keep you from seeing the truth of who you are and trapped in a cage of lack and negativity.

If you find that statement hard to believe, take a truthful look around you. Look at any facet of society and see how it is designed. Look at the results of going to hospital or surviving our education system. These systems harm more than they help and that's the norm. It's become acceptable to hurt others and not care as long as I'm okay.
This book, however is not about cures for society. That is happening already as more and more people awaken to the truth, put down the gun and embrace love as our true nature.

This book is about learning tools that are all about embracing love in every facet of your life. Very simply, if it's not coming from a place of love, why would I feel it? Why would I think it? Why would I do it?

You are a multi-dimensional eternal being of infinite love and light. That is your true nature. It's who you are. When you process, one way to understand what happens is to think of layers of darkness on top of a ball of light. These layers are of different sizes, shapes, thickness and depth. When you remove one you may allow a pocket of light to arise in its place. If that's the case then enjoy the peace, love, stillness that always accompanies it. If darkness is the next layer, it could be any depth, thickness, shape and density. I always advise to continue processing until you come to a place of peace and stillness. As in all things, follow your powerful intuition.

As you process you will experience change in your reality. Now this change may manifest as negativity but ultimately it's all good. All change is a consequence of letting something go. When you remove something you make space for something else to come in.

When you process, you are seeing life through the eyes of love.

Thus as you create, you can only create loving things in your reality. Forget what society has taught you about life. The truth is life's perfect! As in all things, you have the choice to see it that way or as imperfection.

Processing is about transmuting darkness into light, profound, wide sweeping change where you always feel good and better overall, as a result. You may not realise it at the time but as your energies settle you will see that such a change has occurred.

This is where Processing is so powerful. Processing

changes your unconsciousness into consciousness. When you learn to process, you learn to transmute negative to positive, darkness to light and in doing so, you change the way you perceive and therefore how you create your reality.

As energy never dies and will only ever change from one state to another; every time you process, your spiritual energy will increase. Your power to do will have become more.

One of the most fascinating aspects of processing for me is that, whenever I do the work on myself and remember, it's always about me, never about someone else. Whenever I do the work and remove a major, chronic, negative pattern from my energy, that's not the end of the story, so to speak.
Because this is a fractal reality, whatever I remove at a core level is not just gone in this moment, it's gone from my past and from my future. Furthermore, it's been removed from every aspect of this reality.
Which means, when ever I remove major negativity from my energy it's also been taken from all of my family and ancestors.

Now what does that mean? It means that it's gone from my son and his sons, from my father and all of my predecessors. I feel that it's completely gone from my lineage, which is a totally incredible fact that has meant so much for me to know when I've been experiencing "dark night of the soul", which I've been through a few times.
If something can be processed, it should be, as it's negative!

Only negative energy can be processed. There are many ways to process and in this book, I've only briefly covered a handful of methods.

Anything that takes you from fear to love is processing, including when you are fully with grief, sorrow and pain will transmute them to love.
Remember, you are the light and all change is good. So when you are fully with any negativity and bring the light of your consciousness to it, that darkness simply can't be there.

Imagine a pitch black, dark cave, full of negativity and evil. Strike one match in such a cave and the darkness simply vanishes.
You are that light! When you bring your consciousness to any negativity it simply cannot be there.

Such is the power of love. That is your true nature. You are born to Process. You are unconditional love.

ASK GOD FOR HELP

"Ask, and it shall be given you; seek, and ye shall find; knock, and it shall be opened unto you" ~ MATTHEW 7:7

W hen you find yourself in a situation or place in your life where there is just simply overwhelming resistance. Or a time when you are unclear about how to proceed, you have the option to ask for help. Yes, I'm talking about praying.

This may be a time where you are processing or for some reason life is heaping on the portions of perceived negativity.

Who are you asking? God, Buddha, Universe, Jesus? You know the answer to that question. You're asking the same energy so don't worry too much about labels. I know it's tempting to think of God in terms of this or that but God is no thing. If God is anything he/she is unconditional love and a whole bunch of it!

Quantum Physics talks about God as the "Sea of Possibilities" which; as descriptions go is a fairly good one. God is endless, eternal, omnipresent, infinite, love, joy, peace, stillness, perfection, wisdom and indeed a Sea of Possibilities.

This also goes for anything you want in your life. The

Bible states it many times over, "Ask and it shall be given" "Seek and you shall find" While, there's a lot of symbolism in the Bible. There is also a lot of literal truth.

Learn a technique for "Processing" negative into positive. And as you do this you will start to feel more at peace, grounded, alive, in control, abundant and loved. That's your true nature, that's who you are at a core level.

When you have totally removed all the layers of resistance you will come to a place where you are love and light. That is your true essence. The Real you! When you manifest from that place, all that can appear in your reality are Miracles!

Some times as we travel our life path the resistance is such that we may struggle to comprehend, never mind deal with it. First thing to remember is that you are never given anything you cannot deal with. Second thing is that you can always ask for a break in the amount of negativity being released and lessons learned. God is always listening and always there to help. When you ask, it's always answered, always given.

Your Higher Self will help you with anything that is for your Higher good, so best to start on a dialogue with it as soon as possible. The same goes for God. Start a conversation with your creator as soon as possible. Keep focusing on God and watch your reality change. What you focus on is what you bring more of into your life, which is true for all things.

God is pure Omni-present, omnipotent, eternal, infinite, truth, light, wisdom, joy and peace. It's all good my friends. This is who you are at the level of soul.

Keep focusing on anything and it will come to you.
Praying, for me is one of the best ways to process.

We all do what we do to facilitate the path of the one.
We all pray and practice peace, stillness, non-judgment,
gratitude, love, in preparation for the time when Jesus
(the One) will return. Will Jesus appear in a UFO in the
middle of London? Hmm, I would love that, but this is
more about Him being born and cultivated in the heart
and soul of every Man, Woman and Child.
Instead of expecting someone else to appear, become,
Buddha, Mohammad and Jesus, through thought, action
and deed. Become the love you wish for in your life.

MEDITATION

"A mind is like a parachute. It doesn't work if it is not open" ~ *Frank Zappa*

Meditation has been around for thousands of years. Some texts refer to it existing as early as 1st Century BC and most agree to it originating in India. There are many different types of meditation and it's only important to choose one that feels right to you. Don't concern yourself with what others are doing. What resonates with you? This is an important point. As with all things, always follow your intuition in such matters and I have discussed Intuition in another section of the book.

Meditation is what I refer to as the Bed Rock you build your spiritual practices on. Meditate every day. In the morning and later in the evening. Of course more if you are able and any time and any length is better than not at all. Meditation is about being still and looking deep inside. When you do this you are sure to find God after all, God wants you to find Him.

Listed below are just some of the benefits. This list is not exhaustive by any means.

- ∞ Brings body, mind, spirit into harmony
- ∞ Day to day well being
- ∞ Answers to Questions
- ∞ Experience Calmness
- ∞ Provides peace and Joy
- ∞ Helps you discover your purpose
- ∞ Increased self-actualization
- ∞ Increased compassion

- ∞ Growing wisdom
- ∞ Deeper understanding of yourself and others
- ∞ Increased acceptance of oneself
- ∞ Helps with learning forgiveness
- ∞ Changes your perspective for the better
- ∞ Creates a deeper relationship with God
- ∞ Important tool for attaining Enlightenment
- ∞ Allows you to look Inward
- ∞ Helps living in the present moment
- ∞ Creates a widening, deepening capacity for love
- ∞ Discovery of the power and consciousness beyond the ego
- ∞ Experience an inner Knowingness
- ∞ Experience a sense of Oneness
- ∞ Increases the synchronicity in your life
- ∞ Deconstruction of the Ego body – Processing

Meditation is wonderful in many ways and it also is very important in that it allows the practitioner to refine her sensitivity to energy. The stiller you become the easier it is to tune into energy. As time goes by you will find it very useful to tune into finer and finer levels of negativity in your energy bodies.

As part of meditation, I encourage the use of "body scanning". Simply scanning your body for tense muscles and relaxing them. Doing this before and as your fall into meditation will help you drop lower, more rapidly.

As you develop, body scanning can be turned into energy scanning. Scan each energy body in turn, starting from the physical. As you scan, become aware of any resistance, allow it to be, then thank and release it. Remember to breathe love and light after you release. You will know when to do this.

HOW TO MEDITATE

There are many methods of Meditation available. Pick and choose which one suits you best. You may try a few before you settle but it's worth the effort. Meditation should be a daily routine and is always very Simple. Like any of the Tools I refer to, the experience will improve the more you use it. Like a Spiritual muscle, it will become more, the more it is used. Your consciousness is akin to a bright light cutting through the darkness. As you look inwards you transmute whatever darkness you look at. Allow it to be. As in all processing, No judgment, no interaction. There's no need to understand, simply to release. Keep looking and it will disappear; transmuted to love and light.

People come to me and say something like "I've tried meditation. It plain doesn't work!" I ask, "how many times have you meditated?" To which they reply "once". Well, that just is not going to get the job done!

Meditation, like all the tools in this book is a Skill. The more you use it the better the experience will become for you. Love yourself enough to keep at it. The benefits are so powerful. If you were to practice one of the tools referred to in this book. Let it be meditation. Such is it's transformational power. Of course, this is my truth. All truth is relative. Feeling for and standing in your truth is so very powerful.

No one can tell you truth; you have to feel your way.

One method of meditating.

1. Find a quiet place. Sit comfortably. Either in Lotus position or find a comfy chair. It's important to keep your back straight.
2. Close your eyes.
3. Do a quick body scan then, three times, Gently take a deep breath and exhale.
4. Now simply concentrate on your breathing. No need to control it,
5. simply allow your breathing to be natural.
6. Observe your breath as you inhale and exhale.

Begin with 30 minutes and increase over time and as seems appropriate.

This simple technique is somewhere to start from. Explore and experiment. Find the method that is best for you.

As the days go by, supplement meditation and stay grounded with a daily practice of Qi gong, Tai chi or Yoga. Maintain a good diet and positive attitude. Practice kindness and compassion.

Light candles and offer prayers. Choose Love over fear. Choose to see love and Good in everything, situation and person as you will come to see there is only perfection. Everything else is illusion. There is only love.

THE WATCHER OR OBSERVER OF THE MIND

This exercise has been around for thousands of years. It's mainly practiced by Buddhist and Hindu religions and is very powerful. It involves becoming aware of what you think, on a moment to moment basis. Also known as Mindfulness and more readily associated with meditation, it's a state of active open attention in the present moment.
When you're the observer, you monitor your thoughts and feelings from a distance, without judging them good or bad or interacting in any way. A powerful method of living in the moment and when fully rooted in this moment you dissolve all negativity.

Most people spend their life in a state of reaction. They react to everything and anything that happens in their reality, without giving it any or at most little thought. Their powerful mind is running on automatic, reacting to programming from society. Some examples might be, the way your parents and family reacted to triggers, how peers react to stimuli and or reaction to perceived, "good news" or "bad news".

The "Media" is a powerful tool for programming as are all of the main facets of society; Education, Health, Religion, Careers, Armed forces. All these are setup to reinforce negative belief systems. Why is this so? Well, it's that way to prevent you from becoming who you are meant to be; a being of total peace, wisdom, joy and love.

When you are always thinking and feeling negativity you are greatly diminished and easily controlled.

The unobserved mind is the ego. The ego is 100% negative, associated with things, and always in a place of fear.
When you watch your mind and are aware of your thoughts you are in a position to transmute your dark to light. This does not happen all at once but little by little, thought by thought, emotion by emotion.

Simply, when you become aware of a negative thought, and I mean all negative thoughts, that is your ego, and observation of the ego transmutes it to positive energy.

Your ego is devious and will try to trick you into associating with things and roles. Always remember that if you are not thinking love its ego. That realization is enough for the transformation to take place. As you progress with this practice you may notice that negative thoughts become more and more subtle. The ego is always seeking ways to grow and to trick you into identification with things and fear.
Choose to be love moment to moment.

Your goal is to always be in a state of mindfulness, every second of every day, always aware of your thoughts, feelings, emotions and actions. When you first start to practice Mindfulness, it may seem like an impossible task but over time and with only a certain amount of skill you will find that the more you are mindful the more that that repetitive task, the observing, will become part of your energy.

While it may start out as separate from you it will, over time and without effort on your part continue to function automatically. Mindfulness in meditation and mindfulness in day to day activity.

In our society there's a lot of interest in dieting and the next best phase or craze that comes along. Supposedly better than the last one and that will enable us to lose weight and live a healthier life.

As patterns in life usually repeat themselves, the same diets can come around a few times in a slightly different guise, which is fine, but there really is no need to sign up to the latest in dieting.
If you really want to enjoy a healthy body, mind and soul, to be perfectly healthy. All we have to do, is simply, learn to love ourselves.

Whenever you truly love yourself, whatever you eat is going to be perfect for you, no matter what it is. When you are coming from a place of love and in this case loving food for your body. Following your guidance and Intuition, whatever you eat and drink will be perfect for you.

Whenever you love yourself and in turn your body, you will only ever eat the right food for you. You will only drink the right drink for you and exercise using the perfect method for your body. It can be no other way.

So, there's really no need to sign up for a course to help you to loose weight. All you need do is love yourself. By using the tools listed in this book you can learn to love yourself fully and completely in every manner, including what and how you eat.
    Mindfulness, Meditation, Affirmations, Processing and Mirror work. That's all you require.

How do you use these? Well, Meditation allows you to prepare the soil, Affirmations and Mirror work are where you plant the seeds for a good crop of love. All the time being mindful of your thoughts and feelings. Remember to always process using whatever method you prefer.

When you love yourself, your intelligent body will do the rest. Love really is the key to all the joy, peace and abundance in life.

For me this collection of tools is what defines Ascension, and you may or may not have heard the term before.
Ascension for me is about raising your vibration. Ascension is a conscious choice that is always happening, moment to moment, choosing love day after day and staying in a loving, joyous, peaceful, still place, consistently your entire life.

Ultimately everything outside of you is part of the great illusion. Everything begins and ends, is born and dies as part of this dance. When you relinquish things and embrace, silence, peace, joy and the love of God. Not only will your energy and core exist for all eternity but you will be a fully realized being in this life time.

≋

EXPRESSION OF ENERGY

Processing is always about the use of your powerful mind to do, your third eye to observe, and your presence or attention to transmute the darkness. Darkness as referred to here is always fear based and is any degree of negativity.

This like all the tools mentioned will resonate with some of you more than others. Whichever you prefer, please use it often.
You will find that any of the tools can be used whenever you wish but all will be more appropriate at the right time. You will know which to use and when to use it!

Processing can be used to transmute all negative energy, no matter where it is. This could be in your physical, ego, mental, emotional or spiritual bodies.

This method first came to my attention via *Inelia Benz*.

Removing negative energy from your physical body:

Find the emotion or pain and look at it. Simply look and allow it to be there. Observe it with your third eye.
Sit with the negativity and allow it to be. Keep observing.

Can you see what color it is?
Allow that color to expand and grow as big as it can get. Breathe love and light through your crown and then into the negativity.

Ask it to express itself to you. After all, that's its purpose; to express to you.

Allow any feelings, thoughts or emotions to come as they may.

For example: betrayal
Say, "betrayal, you are welcome here"
Can you tell where in the body this word is?

For example: in your right shoulder
Welcome it there and allow it to grow as big as it can get.
Breathe into it and allow it to express to you.
It is welcome here
Let it simply be there

Does it have a feeling attached?
For example: anger
Say, "anger, you are welcome here"
Allow it to be here and let it expand
Ask it to express to you
Then thank it
And release it!

This form of processing is like pruning. Meditation and mindfulness are like cutting the grass to keep the weeds down. Both work but each has a unique strength in different circumstances. Learn to discern which one to use and when.
As with all of the techniques listed in this book, regular practice of this technique is encouraged. Practice until it becomes second nature to you and you are always in a place of stillness and love.

SEEING THE SPACE AND HEARING THE SILENCE

When you can see the space in all things and hear the silence underlying every noise you are focusing in on pure consciousness. This still place is where all wisdom, awareness, joy, peace and love come from. The same facets of eternity and infinity exist inside you as well. As above, so below.

You can practice this during meditation but just as easily it can be practiced and refined when going about your day to day activities.

Look for the space between every noise. The silence that is in, and underlying every sound. Practice this every day and anywhere you are able. You are connecting to Source energy, the place where all things come from, including you.
As you practice this technique, it will have the effect of pulling you into the moment.

When you are fully in this moment your vibration will rise as you will be fully present. When the light burns brightly whatever darkness there may be will be fully and completely transmuted from fear to love.
When you have a consistently high enough vibration, where ever you are, any and all negativity will be transmuted to love. It doesn't matter if it's yours or someone else's. All negativity will be transmuted.

EMOTIONAL FREEDOM TECHNIQUE (EFT)

 Self-help tool for Processing and removing Energy Blocks.

"Remember, we are completely composed of Energy and are connected energetically to everything else in the reality we've co-created."
~ *Paul E. McAtarsney*

What is EFT?

Most people have heard of EFT and are using it in their day to day energy work, maybe for their work with others or simply when they work on themselves. Either way it's a very powerful tool. For me, its main strength is the fact that it works with the subconscious. Why this is important has been discussed in another section of this book. The EFT practitioner works with certain points on the body.

These spots coincide with the Meridians of the body which I will briefly cover in a later section of this book. Tapping on specific acupressure or EFT tapping points, while focusing on a problem or unpleasant feeling or physical sensation, helps to remove the associated emotional element or feeling.
In EFT you use your fingers to lightly tap various spots located on the body and face.

I've used this particular template many times! Try it and let me know how you get on. When I say the script statements I really endeavor to feel what I'm saying with intent and its important to put emotion into your EFT practice.

First things first, gauge the level of your blockage with this neutral statement:

"I am feeling a lot of resistance to (fill in the blank)..............?"

With '0' being false (no resistance at all) and '10' being very true (lots of resistance).

SCRIPT: Clearing Resistance

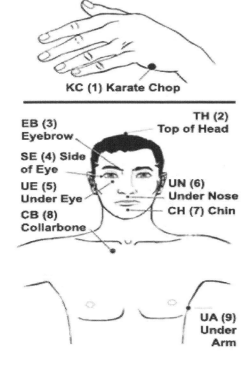

KC – Even though I'm feeling this resistance I choose to love and accept myself

KC – Even though I am feeling resistant to this happening, I deeply and completely accept myself

KC – Even though I'm feeling this resistance I choose to love and forgive myself

KC – Even though I'm feeling this resistance thoughts are going on in my head that tell me to avoid something

KC – and maybe another part of me is saying that that would be good for me

KC – and so I want to clear this resistance

KC – and even though I have this resistance I choose to deeply and completely

KC – love and forgive and accept myself

KC – and anyone else who might of contributed to this resistance

EB – All this resistance

SE – All this resistance

UE – All this Resistance

UN – I can feel it

CH – Sometimes it makes me tense

CB – Sometimes it just makes me feel weak

UA – Sometimes it feels like I'm tired

TH – I'm too tired to do this

EB – I don't have the energy to do this

SE – well that's not true

UE – I'm completely made up of Energy

UN – I'm nothing but energy

CH – I have plenty of energy

CB – I just also have resistance

UA – and I choose to clear it

TH – letting go of this resistance

EB – All this perception

SE – that what I'm resisting

UE – poses some kind of threat to me

UN – I see something as a threat to me

CH – and then I'm stuck

CB – I want this thing

UA – or I want to take this action

TH – but I find myself blocked

EB – because of this perceived threat

SE – because of all this resistance

UE – and I'm releasing that resistance

UN – most of what I'm afraid of

CH – probably isn't true

CB- it's probably not nearly as bad as I'm afraid it is

UA – and maybe it's not bad at all

TH – I choose to question this resistance

EB – I choose to question this threat

SE – what am I really afraid of?

UE – what's stopping me?

UN – with anything that I'm resisting?

CH – I choose to ask myself?

CB – what am I really afraid of?

UA – and I choose to clear that fear

TH – now that I think about it

EB – what I'm afraid of isn't real

SE – clearing this belief that it's something to be afraid of

UE – clearing this fear all the way back to my past
UN – clearing this fear at a cellular level

CH – and letting go of this resistance

CB – so that I can allow myself to take action

UA – so that I can allow really good things into my life

TH – that I've been resisting

EB – I'm question that resistance

SE – and I'm releasing it

UE – releasing it at an energy level

UN – and really setting myself free

CH – setting myself free to move forward

CB – in mind, spirit and body!

Take a deep breath. Check your 0 – 10 level on your statement:

"I am feeling a lot of resistance to (fill in the blank)…………..?"

You will find that the level will have dropped from the original. Keep doing this twice a day and watch the flood gates open!

There are a lot of free resources on the Internet.

As in all of these powerful practices, repetition is key to success.

TONING

Nowadays new and varied energy is coming into our universe every moment. We are all changing, evolving and ascending every second. Everything comes from energy. So anything you do physically can also be done energetically. This works for everything.

Toning has many uses but it is a wonderful way to raise your vibration. In this example, I use the Bija Mantras.
The Bija mantras are a powerful tool for anyone working with energy or seeking enlightenment, peace and health.

I use these set of seven mantras to quickly raise my vibration. You can choose to say them out loud or in your head.

The Bija mantras are seven Sanskrit words that correspond to the seven main third dimensional chakras in the body and are thousands of years old. By chanting them, even just once a day, a person is activating, energizing, balancing and clearing out any blockages that may be in their Chakra System. It is also said that these mantras can be utilized to raise the kundalini energy and work off karma.

The first five are pronounced with a sound similar to *ahhhh*. Om is pronounced like bomb. *All* is pronounced like ball.

As you tone each mantra, in your mind's eye, visualize each Chakra and its associated Color. For example see the root as a vibrant red.
BIJA MANTRAS:

1st CHAKRA (Laaammm)	:RED	:Root	:Lam
2nd CHAKRA (Vaaaaamm)	:ORANGE	:Sacral	:Vam
3rd CHAKRA (Raaammm)	:YELLOW	:Solar	:Ram
4th CHAKRA (Yaaammm)	:GREEN	:Heart	:Yam
5th CHAKRA (Haaammm)	:BLUE	:Throat	:Ham
6th CHAKRA (Oooomm)	:PURPLE	:ThirdEye	:Om
7th CHAKRA (Aaaaallllll)	:WHITE	:Crown	:All

Enjoy, be happy and walk in light always.

BREATHE LOVE AND LIGHT

This can be an underutilized technique, one which is very simple and highly effective. You are 100% energy. Simply, some of your energy is negative, some is positive. Negative energy is heavier than positive energy. When you breathe love and light a few things happen:

1) you replace negative with positive
2) negative energy is displaced, allowing it to manifest at some point and be processed. This may not happen at the time, but will happen at some point.
3) you become more grounded in the moment, and more so when combined with conscious breathing

Breathing love and light is not just for raising your own vibration and like all of the techniques mentioned has many uses. Use your imagination. Be creative, have fun, play and follow your Intuition.

This powerful technique is wonderful when used before meditating, facilitating grounding, centering and relaxation.
Combine techniques. The only limits are the ones that you set.

Breathe in through the nose and out through your mouth. As you breathe in visualize a shaft of Gold light entering your Crown chakra, traveling down to just below your naval.
As you exhale through your mouth, see the love and light passing out through every cell, tissue, and fiber of your

physical body, on out through your ego, mental, emotional and spiritual bodies and then out to the rest of the Universe. The Universe is of course what you are as you are one with all things.

As you breathe, you will feel different sensations, lightly at first, but over time they will grow until you can clearly feel them.
Sensations will range in intensity and duration but as you continue to breathe love and light, stay focused on the feeling rather than any image you may see.

Flooding your whole body with love and light on a daily basis, is a powerful healing practice. As you continue with the practice, include your other energetic bodies.

As you breathe love and light into each body, be aware of any negativity that may arise and process it.
After it's processed continue breathing and processing until all negativity in that body has been transmuted.

Do this for all of your energetic bodies until you can clearly see that they are all filled with what appears to be light.

At this stage you are now working with your light body. Practice daily until you are continually aware of your light body and your illuminated heart.

REIKI

Reiki is a natural system of energy healing. It is done by placing the hands on or near the recipient. The practitioner runs Reiki Energy while placing their hands on or over a series of locations on the recipients' body.
This energy is the life force that permeates the universe.

Practitioners can also work remotely. Remote techniques are usually taught at the second degree level.

The process of doing Reiki treatment is thought of as "laying on of hands" or "spiritual healing" and is considered to be a metaphysical phenomenon.
The simplest definition of the word Reiki is Universal or Spiritual, Rei - Life Force or Energy, Ki.

The Reiki system is a simple and powerful system of energy work that anyone can learn to use for developing physical, emotional, mental and spiritual harmony and wholeness for assisting others.

Reiki functions on the energy body first, usually following the same channels used in acupuncture and acupressure, Qi gong and other traditional Asian Medical and healing modes but not limited to them.
The practitioner uses the Reiki energy to help people move and balance energy, remove blocks and repair tears in the aura and help restore wellbeing.

Advanced practitioners are able to give treatments without touching the recipient and even send treatments great distances, even to people on other continents.

Reiki is not religious. Being attuned to Reiki does not

entail any conversion or adoption of spiritual beliefs or practices from any religion or particular set of beliefs.

Reiki and other energy healing modes will harmonize with most spiritual belief systems that allow for the existence of energy work.

Reiki is a system of energy healing from Japan using methods transmitted to and received by Mikao Usui, at the end of a 21 day fast and meditation on one of Japan's mountains.

Reiki is a simple and powerful system of laying on of hands and remote healing that can transform lives. The Usui System of Natural Healing was introduced to the West by Mrs. Hawayo Takata, from Hawaii, who received Reiki Attunements from Dr. Hayashi.

Dr Hayashi had a Reiki clinic in Tokyo. Mrs. Takata was visiting relatives in Japan and had successful treatments for a chronic illness at Dr. Hayashis' Clinic.

This systems primary goal is to assist people to become enlightened. Physical healing was a side effect rather than the end goal.

The ability to heal physical, emotional, mental, and spiritual imbalances with energy channeled through the hands has been viewed as a rare and mystical gift requiring great spiritual achievement. However this simply is not true. Reiki is almost as easily learned as learning to walk.

Healing energy can be channeled by any one. This ability can be acquired by energetic transmission from one person to another.

These transmissions are called attunements. They remove blocks in the aura and allow the healing energies that surround us to come in through our crown chakra and flow through our bodies and out our hands to where they are needed. This is not the only path for the Reiki healing energies but only the most common or most easily sensed. Others include the eyes and soles of the feet.

Attunements are transmitted and guided by a Reiki Teacher (Reiki Master) into the personal energy field of the recipient. The attunements open the palm chakras and energy channels if this is needed and connect you to the specific Reiki Shakti healing frequencies. The attunements also allow the direction of these energies for specific purposes.

Anyone can get these attunements and channel Reiki, it requires no special abilities and is a dependable way of doing healing treatments for yourself and others.

This form of processing is like pruning. Meditation and mindfulness are like cutting the grass to keep the weeds down. Both work but each has a unique strength in different circumstances. Learn to discern which one to use and when.

Reiki has traditionally been used for treatment of physical issues and to compliment other health treatments and practices. Reiki is not a substitute for medical treatment nor is it a diagnostic system. Reiki is an intelligent energy of love and wholeness.
When you use Reiki you find many more ways to work with and gain value from it. The possible ways and systems for working with universal life force energy are infinite.

Reiki is a form of processing that I've used for some twenty years with great success. As with all forms of healing it can easily and effortlessly be combined with other techniques and you will intuit when to do so.
I advise the user to seek out an experienced Reiki teacher. If for no other reason than that of entrainment. Entrainment has been discussed earlier in the book.

It is also possible to be remotely attuned by a Reiki Master.

As my gift to you I've decided that every reader who purchases this book, will receive a free Reiki attunement.

This will in some way aid the healing that is needed at this time. If you not want to be attuned, deciding so is enough. And so it is.

MYOFASCIAL RELEASE TECHNIQUE

John F. Barnes' Approach

I 've just recently experienced this form of processing which was hugely beneficial to me. John F. Barnes talks about ancient wounds in his books and for me this form of processing was mainly about that. Removing the energy of ancient wounds and past life negative energies.

I've experienced incredible results and feel my personal processing has jumped forward by many years.

I've practiced this with one talented practitioner and can only imagine what a group of such specialists working with me will be like.

Below is more of a technical explanation of the technique. It can be learned for personal use but it may be useful to experience this first with someone who has been taught how to properly use this simple to learn technique.

Fascia is a tough connective tissue which spreads throughout the body in a three-dimensional web from head to foot without interruption.

*Trauma, posture or inflammation can create a "binding-down" of fascia resulting in excessive pressure on nerves, muscles, blood vessels, bones/joints and/or organs. Many of the standard diagnostic tests such as x-rays, myelograms, CAT scans, electromyography, MRI's, etc, do **not** show fascial restrictions. Fascial restrictions can exert approximately 2,000 pounds of pressure per square inch on pain sensitive structures* producing pain, headaches, fibromyalgia and restrictions of motion. The visco-elastic quality of the fascial system causes it to **resist** a _suddenly_ applied force. This explains why the "old form" of MyoFascial release, which was an attempt to force a system that cannot be forced, produced pain and limited results. The John F. Barnes' MFR Approach® consists of the gentle application of sustained pressure into the fascial restrictions. This essential "time element" has to do with the viscous flow and the piezoelectric phenomenon: a low load (gentle pressure) applied slowly will allow a visco-elastic medium (fascia) to elongate/stretch.

The John F. Barnes' MFR Approach® is considered to be safe, gentle and consistently effective in producing results that last. Piezoelectricity, Mechano-transduction, Phase Transition, Chaos and Fractal Theory, and ultimately, Resonance are the key components in changing and improving mind/body health. The importance of sustaining pressure at the restricted barrier to create "phase transition" is paramount for lasting results and stimulates the production of Interleukin 8 which is our body's natural anti-inflammatory. This begins to explain the profound results that one receives when MFR is performed.

Other forms of therapy, massage, modalities and exercise do not engage the fascial restriction long enough to stimulate the phenomena of piezoelectricity, Mechano-transduction, chaos, and phase transition which ultimately leads to resonance. Resonance is essential for the reduction of pain, increase in range of motion, and for **authentic healing** to occur. The stimulation of this phenomenon is significant in creating long-term results.

Piezoelectricity is a Greek word which means pressure electricity. It is a well-known fact that each of our cells are crystalline in nature. When pressure is placed into a crystal, it creates an electrical flow. The sustained pressure of JFB's Approach to MFR coupled with the **essential time element** creates a bio-electrical flow in our body, in other words, **the**

motion of our mind...*which leads into mechano-transduction.*

Mechano-transduction *which is sustained mechanical pressure, can also create biochemical changes within our bodies. Importantly, MFR produces Interleukin 8, our body's own natural anti-inflammatory agent. Research has shown that inflammation is an important part of the healing process. However, when inflammation has been thwarted, it tends to solidify the ground substance of the fascial system which should be fluid. This then blocks healing and over time tends to continue to solidify into crushing restrictions that produce the symptoms of pain, tension and limited range of motion. It is not enough to just treat the effect or symptoms (traditional therapy). Returning to the cause is essential for lasting effects.*

When piezoelectricity and mechano-transduction dove tail together, **Phase Transition** *takes place. This is the phenomena of ice transforming into water. In our bodies, a similar occurrence happens. The solidification of the ground substance becomes more fluid allowing the tissue to rehydrate and to glide taking crushing pressure (approximately 2,000 pounds per square inch) off of pain-sensitive structures.*

Chaos and Fractal Theory: *Everything in traditional medicine and therapy insisted upon order and control. However,* **true growth and healing** *cannot occur in a controlled, orderly way. "Systems Theory" states that nature goes through continuous periods of order, chaos, order, chaos, etc. It is in the "Chaotic Phase" that re-organization occurs. The system then returns to a higher level of order. For Phrase Transition to occur, there is a period of chaos when ice transforms into water or in our body for the solidified ground substance of the fascial system to transform into a more viscous/fluid state. When one person touches another person, their vibratory rates are quite different on the molecular level, however with sustained pressure at the fascial restriction, the vibratory rates will become identical...creating resonance.*

*Resonance is the very essence of JFB's Approach to Myofascial Release. This is what is called a "Release". Release occurs both in the cranial area and throughout the body. Resonance, unfortunately, does not occur in other forms of therapy due to the sheer fact that these other forms of therapy are **too quick**, hence providing only temporary results. The "art" of locating the fascial restrictions, which are totally unique to each individual, combined with the proper amount of sustained pressure will have profound and lasting results!*

Source *http://myofascialrelease.com/*

The mind/body connection in the John F. Barnes Approach to MyoFascial Release is how processing can occur during this therapy. Since there is "no proof" where the mind is located, John F. Barnes believes that our mind is in our fascia.

It is in the motion of the mind that fascial restrictions are found. Once they are found, they can be released. Many memories are released and are dealt with authentically during the MFR release.

Suppressed memories manifest as pain. Processing is necessary to transmute pain into peace, dark to light, fear to Love.

BLESSING

"But I say to you, love your enemies, bless those who curse you, do good to those who hate you, and pray for those who spitefully use you and persecute you" ~ Matthew 5:44

'A Blessing can be defined as a prayer asking for divine favor and protection'
~ Oxford Dictionary

Blessing is a very under rated, simple and under used method to process. When you bless, you heal whatever you bless on every level. Blessing, removes all negativity on and around whatever it is you bless.

Bless everything you can. When you wake in the morning bless your day. Just before you go to sleep, bless your sleep. Bless your family and friends. Bless your meals before you eat. Bless what you drink.

Bless your words before you speak. Bless your thoughts and your feelings. Bless any and all things, people and circumstances, then sit back and watch the transformation.
Maybe you find yourself in a situation where you've drifted apart from a loved one. They, for whatever reason are angry at you. Bless them.

Continue to see the good in them and allow the transformation.

Maybe, you are angry and somehow have chosen fear over love in a situation, try as you might, you just can't choose to go back to a place of love. It happens.

I've been there myself and before learning about processing, I'd have simply gone on suppressing and or ignoring the underlying energy.

When I learned about processing and about the power of Blessings to transform, it totally changed my life. I'd arise in the morning and bless my day. Bless anything that concerned me and then simply allow.

Blessing is very transformative and of course when you bless your enemies, this means that eventually, the energy of an enemy won't exist for you.

Bless you!

SPEND TIME IN NATURE

Everyone intuitively knows there are wonderful health benefits to spending time in nature. We also know how we feel, after a few days inside. Stiff, sore, tired and lethargic.

" *how we feel whenever we spend some fun time outside, walking, hiking, cycling in the green spaces, walking in the wilderness, walking in the mountains. Breathing the fresh air, exercising and creating the chemicals, those good feel natural chemicals in our brain.*

There's also scientific research and studies that show that a large range of illnesses are positively affected by spending time and being outside and spending time in nature. Everything, from Asthma, depression, general health, heart health, Obesity, Stroke, Stress and general well-being are all positively affected by being outside.

Some hospitals have noted that patients whom have a view of trees and or the outside tend to heal faster than those who sit and stare at a wall all day.

There's also been research that shows people are affected by the number of trees that are in their community. Fewer trees have been linked to greater deaths due to lower respiratory track and cardiovascular illness. "

Above taken from the *American Journal of Preventative Medicine 2013.*

People who live in communities that are walk able, have access to bike trails and are near to parks and green space generally have higher levels of health, compared to those individuals who live in communities lacking those same services.

Energetically, when we connect to the energies in nature, we are connecting to the pulse of Mother Nature or Gaia. There's a core vibration or pulse that we can connect to, and when we do that it has huge health benefits.

Nature also provides lessons how to behave, how to interrelate, how to be still and how to not interact. How not to judge and about cooperation. Nature is all about cooperation. There are very few cases where animals and vegetation don't cooperate in some way. It's their core nature to cooperate. Nature always cooperates.

There's a great lesson for us as a society. Instead of competing and fighting, we should all be working together. Sharing what we know, do and have with each other. Want to learn about spirituality and love?
Observe and be in Nature.

ENERGETIC DEFENSE

This is a topic that I've had to feel into considerably more than any other. The main question for my self was to write about it or not. The reason shall be explained a wee bit later on in this section. Basically, defense is about stopping other people, Entities, any source sending you negative energy, or you maybe are in a geographical area which contains a lot of negativity. Defense is about preventing that energy affecting your energy.

Also, someone may attack you energetically. An attack may be as simple as an individual thinking about you in a negative way or a couple of people gossiping about you. You are energy and so are they.

They are powerful creators as we all are, so when they send that energy you will feel it and as a consequence, it can have serious effects on your energy and on your long term health, in general, if you don't prevent it.

This is a good example of refining your sensitivity to energy to the extent that you are able to feel the change of energy and take action. I usually start by asking the question," is this coming from me?" or "where is this coming from?"

Depending on the answer, I take loving action. Remember that, in this example, these people may not realize what they are doing or the harm they cause. It's simply something, their Mum did, and or their friends do, something society has taught them.

As with all processing, it's not important to know why

they are doing it, it's only necessary to remove the negativity by taking action.

So now you feel this energy. You have an intuitive guide, a nudge that this is happening now. Don't ignore it, take action.

You can start by asking the Angels to protect you from negativity. Or use the following method.

One method is to visualize a shield around you and as you do, you will immediately feel that the negativity has stopped. It can't get past your shield. No negative energy, what so ever can get past the shield. The only thing that is allowed to pass is positive energy. There are many ways to stop negativity and some examples are, visualizing yourself inside a rubber suit, behind a shield, in a diving bell, in a bubble. There is an infinite number of ways you can imagine to shield yourself from negativity, so, have fun doing so. Play with it.

An addition to some sort of shield is the use of a mirror to reflect the negativity back to the source, so that the harm it does may be felt by whomever is sending it.
If someone is gossiping, this might be felt by a realization that this isn't a positive loving way to talk about someone.

One last, housekeeping thing to do, is cut all etheric cords. Using your mind's eye, choose to see all cords that connect to you and simply cut them. If you find that you can't cut them, ask the angels for assistance. Arch Angel Michael is wonderful for cutting cords. I always cut all cords as any that are meant to reattach will. Let's say you cut a cord that is attached from an important relationship, it will simply re-attach after it's cut.

Cutting cords should be a daily practice as it helps you retain your energy until you are in a position to not need this practice. Now, after raising shields and cutting cords, you can choose to send love and light.

Feel the love in your heart, smile and consciously send Love. Sending love and light, blessing these beings, is always a wonderful healing practice and one I advise finishing up with. You can do all or part of this, while driving in the car, at work or in other activities. Simply, say or think something like, "shields up" and it's done. That will keep you protected and you can choose to do the rest at a later stage.

The mechanisms that can be used for energetic defense are not limited to those listed here. There are many other ways, including the use of a pendant or crystal worn around the neck or carried somewhere on the person, like a ring or in your pocket.

A five sided Pentagram offers really good protection and should have one of the angles pointing upwards, otherwise it has a very different meaning.

Black Tourmaline is my number one choice for protection when using crystals. It should be noted that if you are working with any crystals, it's important to clear them of negativity on a regular basis and crystals should be asked on an individual basis, if they are willing to work with you. You may find that some will not want to work with you when asked. How do you ask them? Simply, bring yourself to a still place and ask the crystal if it wants to work with you. Be honest about the answer you receive. If that crystal doesn't want to work with you, there will always be one that does.

As I mentioned earlier, there's a debate about whether or not there's a need to defend yourself in the first place? Does the light require shielding from the darkness? I don't believe that we do. When you are fully aware of your power as pure love, then no one and nothing can harm you. There's no need for shielding or protection of any kind.

These defense tools are only necessary while you transition from mainly dark to mainly light.

One of the most fascinating aspects of processing for me is, that, whenever I do the work on myself and remember, it's always about me, never about someone else. Whenever I do the work and remove a major, chronic, negative pattern from my energy; that's not the end of the story, so to speak.

Because this is a fractal reality, whatever I remove at a core level is not just gone in this moment, It's gone from my past and from my future. Furthermore, it's been removed from every aspect of this reality.

Which means, whenever I remove major negativity from my energy it's also been taken from all of my family and ancestors.

Now what does that mean? It means that it's gone from my son and his sons, from my father and all of my predecessors. I feel that it's totally gone from my lineage, which is a completely incredible fact that has meant so much for me to know when I've been experiencing "dark night of the soul"; which I've been through a few times.

Raising your vibration a choice at a time, moment to moment. The thing is, until you attain that knowing, and you get that knowing by being love. Until then, why should you allow this to happen? Why should you allow someone else's careless actions and thoughts to harm you in any way? You have a right to be in a loving, joyous, peaceful energetic place. A right to look after your energy and allow others to do the same.

ʒ

DWADLE

This is a technique used by *Burt Goldman*. You may know him as the *American Monk*. It's one of the simplest of techniques and yet so effective. I've used it on myself many times with great success.

It works like this. Take a pencil and a piece of paper. Draw what looks like a stick figure. Nothing elaborate. Do not include details like eyes, mouth, eye brows, ears or any other detail.

It's simply an outline of the head, arms, from the head down to the groin area and then two legs, no need for hands or feet. Very basic. That's a Dwadle.

How to use a Dwadle is by first finding out what it is that requires healing. Let's say it's a sore head.
In the part of your Dwadle that depicts the head, roughly draw some lines to highlight the area where the soreness is and that's it!

Get the person with the sore head to run his eyes along the peripheral of the Dwadle. Just follow the outline of it while thinking of his head. Only think of the head, not the pain. Do this for a few minutes. And that's it!

If this is for you, then you do the same. Simply look at the outline of the Dwadle.

Pick a spot to start and follow the outside line of the stick figure for a couple of minutes, thinking of your head, not the pain, just the head.

If you want, before you start, check the intensity of the head ache on a scale of 1 to 10, with 10 being intense and 1 being very mild.

Re-check the scale after a few minutes of processing. Repeat above until the pain has decreased to a low enough level.

Incredibly simple technique that works. Thank you Mr. *Goldman*.

EYE THERAPY

Eye therapy, or Hand-Eye therapy is a wonderful method of processing. I've used this on occasion to quickly remove memories, ways of thinking and unwanted patterns from my mind. It's also a powerful tool in helping others.

Before you start, ask the person you are working with to remember a traumatic experience.

Ask them how they feel on a scale of 1 to 10; ten being very upset and one being totally at peace.

Now, ask them to relive the experience in as much detail as possible and as they do to look at and follow the tips of your fingers.

Hold your hand in front of their face and move your fingers in a figure eight, Torus shape. As they watch, ask them to stay focused on their memory.

After a couple of minutes ask the person you are working with to rate their memory on the scale of 1 to 10. You will notice that the number has reduced. Repeat the above process until the number is low enough. The user will know what that is.

Eye therapy can be used on yourself by simply remembering an experience, gauging it on the 1 to 10 scale and moving your eyes in a figure eight pattern. You can also open and close your eyes as you move them.

Continue until the number on the scale is low enough and or the memory has been completely removed or at a low enough level to be acceptable. This easy to learn technique is highly sought after by many professionals, including physiologists and physiatrists.

You could attend a weekend course and spend thousands but what I've described is more or less how to use it.

REMOVAL OF ENTITIES

This one has been huge for me recently. We are multi-dimensional being of love and light energy. Contained within are layers upon layers consisting of negativity and love.

These layers are random in size, density, shape and thickness. This adds an element of unpredictability to processing. I seldom know what's being released until it appears.
What's been happening lately is, as I process and transmute; the more I become conscious of entities that should be released.

What do I mean by the word entities? Well, I mean spirits of beings past. Lost souls that somehow are in my energy and the more I process and transmute negative to positive the more spirits are coming to the forefront to be released and assisted back to the light. I say *should* in the paragraph above, as most want to go; some that have been there for a long time do not.

There are two techniques I've been using to release entities from my energy, namely MyoFascial Release and Expression of Energy; although other processing techniques can be used.

I start by asking my higher Self

   1) are there any entities in me?
   2) how many entities are there?

Then I ask say:

" In the name of Jesus the Christ. I command you (insert number here) to leave me now gently and forever" – repeat 3 times

"I fill the void with the love and light of the Holy Spirit"

"I ask that Archangel Michael bring you all back to the light"
"Thank you Archangel Michael... it is done"

Repeat until you get an answer of zero entities.

I've been practising this technique for a few years now and find it very effective. It can be used as many times in the day as you remember.

Like all of the tools mentioned, you will find a time and a place when this tool is more appropriate than other ways of processing.

It occurred to me not to include this information as it may be somewhat shocking for my readers but it has been my experience and so in the spirit of truth and light the information has been included.

From my own experience this method of releasing entities is highly effective.

AFFIRMATIONS & MIRROR WORK

We are very powerful, multi-dimensional being of love and light. We, are responsible for everything that happens in our life and as I discussed in a previous section, we create our reality mainly from the sub conscious.

Now when I say "we create our reality", that's not just some wishful thinking on my part, that's the truth. You create everything in your reality, whether, negative or positive.

Everything that comes to you, does so because you create and pull it to you. No one else or situation or thing is responsible. You are!

The words you use on a day to day basis reflect what you are thinking and feeling. This in turn shows you in general, what you are creating.

If you are thinking, from a place of lack and from a place of "nothing good ever happens to me" or "I can't have that", then good will seldom happen and you will never have whatever it is you wish to see appear in your life.

Basically, when you think in a negative way, you will eventually have negative feelings, which in turn will manifest as illness in your body and or conditions in your life and in your reality.

Want to change your reality and life circumstances? Change the way you think and how you relate with it.

Instead of negative thoughts, choose positive ones. Instead of looking at life from the "pint always half empty" perspective, choose the "pint half full" view point.

Easier said than done you may say, but it's as easy as you want it to be; when you decide that's what's going to happen.
With the assistance of this tool you can learn to change what's being created via your subconscious.

Okay, so how do you do that?
One of the ways is to use affirmations. Affirmations don't have to be complicated and in fact I advise that you keep them simple.

For example:
   I am Love
   I am abundant
   I am excited and confident
   I love myself
   I love everyone
   I love my life

Thank you for:

   this productive positive day
   all the abundance in my life
   all the love in my life

These are simple sentences that you repeat over and over until they replace any negative patterns in your subconscious.

Pick one from the list above and repeat it ten times out loud as you look into a mirror. You ideally should do this twice a day and or as you walk past a mirror.

You can devise statements to suit your needs. Let's say you want to improve your ability to give. You might say "I am generous".   Whatever it is, by reprogramming your subconscious with the use of affirmations you can change how you, think, feel and create.

You replace any negative, patterns in your reality with positive patterns.

Remember, no one else can do this for you and if you allow others to tell you how to live, love and exist, you are giving away your power.
You are a very powerful being of love and light. Choose to take back your power and create only from a place of love.
These techniques, these tools, are powerful by themselves but used in combination are so much more powerful. It really is a simple matter of learning how to use each tool to a reasonable standard and then combining them. Just use your imagination. There's no right or wrong here.

For example, using affirmations with mirrors and combining that with mindfulness. You might affirm " I am abundant" as you look into your eyes in the mirror and as you are smiling and feeling good about the statement.

This in itself is powerful but if at the same time you are mindful of your energy and feelings, and use that technique at the same time, you can monitor your energy for any resistance, and therefore, any negativity to that statement. The recognition of that resistance is enough to remove it at that moment. Like all processing, you may not remove it totally the first time, but keep going and eventually it will be totally gone from your energy.

Processing, and therefore, transmuting negative to positive energy by using any of the exercises listed before meditation will enable the practitioner to start the meditation from a deeper, calmer, stiller place. There won't be as much mental noise, if any at the start of meditation.
Starting your meditation from here is incredibly powerful and loving.

JOURNALING

The benefits of examining and fully being with whatever has happened in your day are very clear. After all, we are talking about processing when we bring our presence to any situation, thing or circumstance.

You could simply have a gratitude journal, where you list everything that you're grateful for in the day and in your life but writing down everything that's happened during your day, might help you in tracking patterns and trends that maybe should be changed. When you are aware of trends in this way it facilitates a course of action for certain situations and circumstances.

Benefits include

Clarification of your thoughts and feelings:
Writing down your thoughts and feeling, just as they are is a wonderful way to understand what's going on in your world.

Know yourself better:
As you write, it will become clear what events in your life you don't like and which ones you prefer.

Reduce stress:
Writing down your emotions like anger and frustration, for example, will assist you in coping with them each time they are encountered.

Solve problems more effectively:
Journaling is a wonderful tool for unlocking your intuitive side.

You can if you want, type up your journal on the computer, but the whole idea of journaling is that handwriting keeps things spontaneous and also gives you clues about your emotional state. If you're anything like me, you'll be able to tell what you're feeling just by looking at the condition of your writing at that time.

Take your journal everywhere. Include everything that's happened in your day. It's a repository for all of the things that interest and inspire you as well as anything that troubles you. Whatever is important or interesting, write about it.

Journaling is also a great way to hone your creativity and passion without feeling censured and criticized in any way.

A Journal is completely private and should only be seen by the author.

I've added a few blank pages at the end of the book for the reader to play around with journaling and or make notes on their day to day experience with processing.

AN EXPERIENCE AFTER A PROCESSING SESSION

This is what I experienced after a particularly intense processing session. I can best describe it as an out of body experience and a message about my work on the earth plane at this time.

Rows and rows of steps up to the clouds. I progress up them very slowly reaching the cloud line. As I pass through, I see above me more rows of steps and a cloud line in the distance. I press on. Not walking, flying upwards. Still it's a long way to go. I ask for assistance.

My Guardian angel swoops in from the right side takes my arm and we zoom upwards at a much accelerated rate.
As we pass through the clouds, I see more steps and clouds far above.
Another Green winged angel joins us from below my feet and we continue upwards, through the cloud base.
As we pass through, a Blue winged Angel joins us on my left side. Still higher we go passing through the next layer of clouds.
A Golden Angel is now in front of me.
Between them the angels carried a scroll, a sword, a shield, a laurel, a cloak and a horn of Cornucopia. All made from gold.
I also notice a cord that runs from me back down to the earth plane.

We fly very quickly to the next layer of clouds and stop.

The Angels ask me if I wish to pass through. If I do I will not want to return they note.

I look around at each although my attention is on the glowing cloud just above me. All I have to do is reach out. I think of Marge, and the work we have to do at this time, and decide to stay on earth as a vessel of God's Will.

I find myself fully re-instated in my body, lying where I started, in my room.

LESSONS

ALL CONNECTED

What is a lesson? A lesson for me is a set of circumstances that bring you to a pivotal point in your life, where you get to choose between fear and love. There are small lessons and there are large ones. If we don't learn the small ones, they get bigger over time until the universe delivers a lesson we can't ignore, and it's then we really feel it! It's always better to notice negative patterns before they manifest into something large.

Whenever something is happening to me that means it's also happening for everyone else as well and I know this is so because we are all connected.

What do I mean by that? I may find that today I'm learning a lesson on trust. That means we are all learning a lesson on trust.

We may not all be learning the lesson in the same way or for the same length of time but we all learn it to some extent or we choose not to learn it at that time but maybe the next.

Lessons for me take as long as they take but to totally learn a lesson can take moments, months to years or maybe life times. When you learn a lesson, you don't have to go through it again. You've learned that particular one, so why would you have to undergo it again?

Why would you have to endure something again if you've learned from the experience?

The whole idea is that you've learned to see past the illusion of fear to the truth of love. Next time that circumstance comes to you again, and it's likely that it won't as you will see through the illusion. From my experience once I've truly learned a lesson it never re-appears. That is so because the pattern I was in is broken and never again will I experience it.

Lessons are not the only way I know we are all connected. Most people can recall a time when they've been thinking of someone they may not have seen for a long time and that person phones them or they accidentally meet or someone else mentions their name in conversation.

This reality is a classroom where you get to learn lessons on love. The quicker you learn your lessons the sooner you get to evolve.

So, instead of fear, moment to moment, choose Love.

UNDERGROUND

At one time, I lived in a city in the UK called London. London is a large metropolitan city of some millions of people and there's many different ways of commuting and traveling throughout it's great boundaries. These methods include Car, Bus, Overhead Rail, and Underground Rail.

Now the underground railway system is the one I want to talk about as there's one particular area in London and station I go to on a regular basis, via underground.

I come out one exit and walk to a down ramp that takes me to an underpass for a busy road that I need to bypass. Normally, I would exit the Station and turn left. Walk for about five minutes until I come to the ramp which takes me to the road underpass and then carry on to my destination.

The more I used this particular underground station, the more aware of a voice growing louder and louder asking, "what happens if I turn right instead of left?"

When I did this one day, I found that the station building itself was built on a circle and turning right took me to my destination much quicker.

And so it is, with using the tools in this book, as you use them, you raise your vibration and tap in to your inner wisdom. As you do so, what once was hidden becomes visible to you. What once was unclear, you see and understand.

As you read these passages, you may ask, "Why didn't you turn right in the first place?" Well, at the time everyone else was going left and it seemed like the thing to do was go that way. It can be the same in day to day life.

At times, it may seem that the right thing to do is to keep going the way you always have and or to keep following the crowd but when you follow your intuition you will see more options that more suit your journey and purpose.

Keep refining your energy and choosing to come from a place of love in all things and your life will change to reflect your energy enhancements. This book is merely a starting point for you. Find your own tools, your own ways of processing dark to light. Moment to moment choose love.

LESSONS AND THE SEVEN ESSENE MIRRORS

"From the perspective of the ancient Essenes, every human on the earth is an initiate in the Mystery School that we call Life. Whether they are conscious of it or not, every human will experience in the presence of others mirrors of themselves in that moment. If we have the wisdom to recognize those mirrors, we may accelerate the evolution of emotion and understanding."   ~ Gregg Braden

The Seven Essene Mirrors are a way of understanding how this process works. We can use what seem to be negative experiences as stepping stones to healing and empowerment.

The Essenes were members of an austere Jewish group in the 1st century BC and the 1st century AD. Most of them lived on the western shore of the Dead Sea. They are identified by many scholars with the Qumran community that wrote the documents generally referred to as the Dead Sea Scrolls.

FIRST MIRROR reflects to us that which we are. What am I sending out into the outside world right now in the present moment? It is something we ourselves are doing or where we ourselves have been in error or wounded.

SECOND MIRROR reflects to us that which we judge. It is something we have an emotional charge with, something we have either been wounded by in the past and have not forgiven. It is good to discern; however if we judge and condemn with an emotional charge, we will attract exactly what we judge into our lives. What am I judging in the present moment?

THIRD MIRROR reflects back to us something we lost, or gave away. When we see something we love and desire in another, it is often something we have lost or given away in our own lives. Every relationship is a relationship with self and often we try to reclaim what was lost or we gave away as a child. It could be sexual attraction and feeling of being in love, having chemistry or joy, innocence, honesty and integrity and courage or love.

FOURTH MIRROR reflects back to us our most forgotten love. This could be a way of life, a lost or unfinished relationship. What are my attachments and addictions, for which I am willing to give away cherished things and people just to accommodate them?

FIFTH MIRROR of my own parents and what is my relationship to the male and female divine principle. We also often become them acting out the same unhealthy and healthy patterns we learned as a child.

SIXTH MIRROR reflects back to us the Dark Night of the Soul. This is when we meet our greatest challenges, our greatest fears and have been gathering the tools and understandings in life to confront them. God never gives us any more than we can handle and we have a choice, fear or love.

SEVENTH MIRROR reflects back to us our self-perception. Others will perceive and treat us according to how we perceive and treat ourselves. If we have a low self-esteem and do not acknowledge our wisdom and beauty, others will not acknowledge them. By what external measure am I judging myself and my successes? This mirror shows us that everything that happens is perfect and so are we.

If we are angry, bitter and unloving to others, they in turn will often reflect that back in the same way. If we change our perception of ourselves, we change the world. Coming from a place of love in all things is the only way.

Over the years understanding Mirrors has proven a powerful tool for comprehending how I interact with my reality. Most people are aware of the First but not many have knowledge of the other Six.

As you become more aware; learn to refine your energy and sensitivity as new levels of wisdom and understanding open up. Mirrors powerfully reflect our state of awareness. Helping us in identifying lessons yet to be mastered and those we already have had success with.

When you have learned a lesson, you don't have to learn it again. This process and time it takes are as different as there are unique things in the Universe.

There's never a rush to learn as you have all the time you require, Now.

The Essenes very wisely recognized that life is like a classroom and we are at once a teacher and a pupil, as is everyone else that we meet in our lives. At once, teaching us something and learning from us. While this reality may look simple, and it is, as how can perfection not be? It's also very intricately and finely woven together levels of subtle energy.

This is the same for the lessons we receive on a moment to moment basis. So much so, that our minds can't understand but our being can. The Essenes could see this and refined the level of understanding of this interaction into Seven Mirrors.

If the reader could understand all seven levels and then use those levels on a day to day basis, to understand his interactions with life; it would have a very powerful effect on his reality.

Understanding the first mirror is a wonderful step for everyone to grasp. That everyone that comes to you is mirroring what is already inside you.

Teachers come in many forms. Every person, animal and situation is a teacher. As is every book, CD, sound or smell.

Teachers don't have to be a person; teachers come in many forms, including dreams. Stay open to possibilities.

This classroom never ends. It's here to assist you in the realization of your true self and your true self is love.

The simple realization that everything is your teacher is a

powerful lesson in itself.

The beautiful thing about lessons, is once it's learned, you don't have to learn it again. Why would you, it's been learned? There's no point in relearning something you've already learned.

Lessons will come to you as small lessons. Something that you will hardly notice. Maybe at first you might feel a twitch in your body, which you ignore. Then one day, you have a pain in your side, which you ignore. This continues until you arrive in hospital and have to re-assess your life.

Best to catch a lesson when it's relatively small and easy to resolve. If you ignore a lesson, whatever it may be, over time, it will grow until you have to deal with it. So, learning to recognize patterns and deal with the small lessons in life before they grow larger is a very valuable skill.

River of life flows endlessly through the Universe and as you flow along with this river, this life force; you can change your direction by the choices you make at any given moment.

A fearful thought will take you in one direction and a positive thought will steer you in another direction. There are important things to understand about what's happening as you go through life. Whenever you choose a fearful thought or a fearful decision, you might find that you are in a circumstance of more fear. Or you find that your life purpose has been delayed and you arrive into a stagnant area in your life of no growth. Much like getting pulled into an eddy of a river.

You end up here because of a negative pattern that until you learn the lesson from, you are destined to remain in.

You could be there, for weeks, months, years, or you could learn the lesson in minutes and move on down the river. It's up to you. You have all the power.

Remember that all change is good, no matter what it may look like on the surface. It's good simply because it happened. Because it happened makes it the right thing. The good news is that there are other benevolent forces at work in this river that guide you and assist you in staying on your path and reaching your goal.

The Angels, for example, are always there, helping us in many ways. These beautiful energies are always watching, always present, always loving and will never intervene unless you ask.

It's important to pray and ask for help when you feel it's required. There is so much love and abundance for you. This is not a lack universe, it's an abundant one. So, put your lack thinking to one side and pray and believe in a loving abundant universe. This universe and reality is not about lack, separateness and fear, it's about abundance, cooperation and love.
     Learn the lessons quickly and move on to bigger and better in your reality.

As we travel through life, attaining new levels of acceptance and wisdom, we know that at the end of the river, awaits Ascension. The choice is either Ascending in this life time or it's Ascension we will experience whenever we pass over, from this mortal realm to the etheric one.

OLD LADY DRINKING TEA

In a café drinking my tea it just happened I was sat across from an older lady. Suddenly, I was aware of her old dry skin. Her gray hair, her demeanor was so old. She reeked of old age. I felt waves of disgust and anger. How could she have the front to be out in public like that?

Memories of years gone by flooded my awareness. How older people had treated me as a child. How they looked down on me. How they belittled me in order to make themselves feel better. Some way for them to feel more than they were feeling at the time.
How could she have done that to me?

A few moments passed and I realized what was happening. This beautiful soul was mirroring back to me in a most expert way, my own judgment and fear.

Judgment; the one thing that I'd been focused on removing from my own energy. The thing that I was so afraid of in my daily interactions with others, being judged. Then the other thing my ego was afraid of, getting old and dying.

 I sat in silence, observing this soul in all her beauty and perfection.
My ego, fearful and alone. Still a thing of beauty but never to be aware that it's connected to all things.

Die? How can infinite, eternal, multi-dimensional beings of love and light ever die? Thankful for this processing opportunity I smiled.

What do I mean by the above statement? Well, you are a multi-dimensional being of light. A being that always has been and always will be. You are a spark of God and as such you have control over everything in your reality. You exist above any preconceived boundaries you may have about this lifetime.

You came here to grow by experience, to facilitate the expansion of the Universe and all that is.
You accomplish this by walking your path. This is your personal unique journey and can only be completed by you.

Everyone has a path but none are the same, even though they all lead to the same place. What place is that? That's a place of total enlightenment, a place of Peace, Joy and Love.

Why would you want to go there? Well, you're going there one way or the other. When you pass over, you'll be there but why choose a life of pain and negativity when you can create Heaven on Earth NOW?

Come from a place of love in everything. What I mean by that is this:

With everything in life, you have a choice on how to interact, and that choice is fear or love. In this reality you simply get more of what you choose and or focus on. When you choose anything fear-based you will create more negativity. But when you choose love, you will simply create more love in your reality.
Choose to live the life of your dreams.

Processing is very loving as you love yourself enough to transmute negativity to light, fear to love.

CONCLUSION

There is a reality you are not aware of as yet. It's a reality of peace, joy and love, of which abundance in all things exists and more, is your natural divine right as a Son of God.

This book is essentially about Processing and about what that means to each faithful practitioner. The benefits, of which there are many, are listed and suggestions on how to incorporate these techniques into your day to day life are offered.

The reader is not limited to the techniques in this book and the author encourages him to discover his/her own techniques for processing and share them with anyone who is interested.

The tools in this book can be used separately or they can be used collectively. I encourage you to learn each one until you have attained a high level of competence and then when you feel confident, to play around with combinations. You may get intuitive nudges, and when you do, follow them.

Awareness is but a change in perspective. You get to choose, moment to moment which reality you abide in. As you Process, your awareness will change, if that is your desire and your truth and inner wisdom revealed.

At the beginning of this book I talked about being truthful. Now is the time to be truthful in every aspect of your life. It's about shining the light of your consciousness on every facet of your reality.

Taking responsibility and ownership of everything that is you and remembering that everything is you. Being grateful for the good and the perceived not so good. Looking at all aspects of your life with integrity and truthfulness and always from a place of love.

Speak your truth, stand in your power, be one hundred percent honest with yourself and others. This doesn't mean you are rude or hurtful, it means always coming from a place of love.

Discern what is right for your advancement and learning and what or who is too destructive to continue on your journey with.
Having learned the lessons, we gladly leave all behind that no longer serves us, in the knowledge that all is as it should be. From a place of awareness we now see that all is indeed as it should be.

Indeed, we are here at this time to experience and express divinity. You are God, we are all one, all that separates us is only a facet of illusion. The wide spread illness that presently afflicts mankind.

There is a cure and that cure is you. When you choose love, no matter what, you tilt the balance back to the light. When you transmute negative to positive, by whatever means, you make that change for all of us and like Jesus, what you do is now available in the collective consciousness for everyone to do.

As more and more of us choose love, more and more put aside fear and embrace the truth of who and what we are, the reality of humanity will once again be Love.

Everyone you interact with at this time is part of your soul family. The members of our soul family, while all they do is done in love, do not always provide us with pleasure and joy, and sometimes they come to provide us with difficulty and challenges so we can learn and become more. As our awareness develops, so we recognize our soul family members and the gifts of love they truly bring us.

This truth always reminds me of a short story by

Nigel Edwards Walker

called **THE SOUL IN THE CAVERN**

There was a soul whose time was coming to take a human birth, so it went to the great cavern where all such souls go. In the cavern were hundreds of thousands of souls, each manifesting a small blue flame. When it's time finally came, the soul stood up and said "My time has come to take human carnation, for I have work to do and many lessons to learn. In my life as a human I shall need family and loving friends to help me, to love me and to nurture me. Who will be my family on Earth?" A ripple flickered across the thousands of flames and, shortly, a few stood forward and said "We do not know you, we have not met you before and we are strangers, but being kind and giving love is a pleasant and easy task. We will be your friends and family on Earth."

The soul spoke out again and said "And on Earth I shall need teachers, people to guide me, to correct me and to discipline me. Who will be my teachers?"

Again a ripple went out around the assembled flames, and a group came forward and said "We have known you in other lives and we have grown to respect you and like you. We will take on the task of being your teachers in life."

And, a third time, the soul spoke out and said "On Earth, if I am to learn the greatest lesson of all, the lesson of humility, tolerance under provocation and to love those who hate me, I shall need people to hate me and to do violence towards me. Who will do this for me? Who will be my enemies?

There was a long pause in the cavern until, at last, a small group came forward and said "We are your soul group, we have known you over aeons of time and your growth and your learning are as dear to us as our own. This is the most delicate and difficult task and, if you are to be hurt and abused, it would be better done by loving friends. We will be your enemies on Earth."

Learn to judge less and discern more. As indeed what you do to someone else you truly do to yourself. Imagine a world where we have expanded the meaning of our family to those with whom we are not blood related. One where we are all part of a larger family. A soul family that is made up of those we now recognise as those we made plans and agreements with before arrives on this earth plane.

We all did this before we came into this lifetime for the purpose of learning lessons and helping each other in the expansion of consciousness. Everyone you interact with and is experiencing the same reality as you do, has the very same love at their core.

Your time on this mortal plane is about choosing Love in all things. In this classroom, everything that comes to you, does so as a lesson. Depending on your response, you may have to learn the lesson again or move on to the next level.
See, you have all the power over your life. Anything else is deception and illusion.

You can have, do and be anything you wish and, in truth, you already are doing these things, you're just not aware of it yet because you have been trained by society to be more aware of the dark than light. More aware of fear than Love.
With the tools in this book, now in an empowered position, choose to escape the nightmare reality and live the life of your dreams.

It is my intention that each reader, understanding this truth and the daily negative programming that each one of us is born into, step into their power and put together his/her own "Tool belt" of Love.

≋

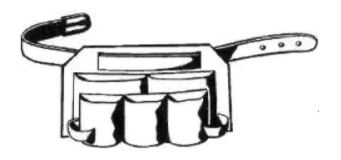

ABOUT THE AUTHOR

Paul has been involved in healing for some 20 years. Over that time he has developed skills in the following:

Spiritual Teacher

Ascension Coach

Reiki Shiki Ryoho Master Teacher

Negative Pattern De-programmer

Paul also uses E.F.T, Toning, Meditation, Reflexology, amongst many others to enhance his work.

"Some years ago I worked in the corporate world but found the conflicts of my profession with the human race and healing growing daily. I endured but eventually gave in to the will of Spirit and arrived in Ireland. There my life was transformed, leading to the writing of this book."

JOURNAL

48379080R00078

Made in the USA
Charleston, SC
02 November 2015